Robin Hood

Level 2

Retold by Liz Austin
Series Editors: Andy Hopkins and Jocelyn Potter

Pearson Education Limited
Edinburgh Gate, Harlow,
Essex CM20 2JE, England
and Associated Companies throughout the world.

ISBN 0 582 421195

This edition first published 2000

NEW EDITION

Copyright © Penguin Books Ltd 2000
Illustrations by Chris Ryley
Cover design by Bender Richardson White

Typeset by Pantek Arts Ltd, Maidstone, Kent
Set in 11/14pt Bembo
Printed in Denmark by Norhaven A/S, Viborg

Published by Pearson Education Limited in association with
Penguin Books Ltd, both companies being subsidiaries of Pearson Plc

For a complete list of the titles available in the Penguin Readers series please write to your local
Pearson Education office or to: Marketing Department, Penguin Longman Publishing,
5 Bentinck Street, London, W1M 5RN.

Contents

Introduction

Lord Gamwell followed the man to the middle of Sherwood Forest. There, in the spring sunshine, he saw his daughter. He also saw a baby boy in her arms. Joanna looked up at her father and smiled.

'This is Robin, your grandson,' she said.

Robin Hood was born in the forest, and the forest was his home for much of his life. His story is hundreds of years old. At that time, in England, many Saxon people lived in small villages on the lands of important Norman lords (from Normandy, now in France). Other people lived on church lands. Life was hard for these villagers because they had to give money and food to their lord and to the church.

So village people loved to hear stories about Robin Hood. Robin Hood was clever, strong and brave. He loved adventure, and he was the best fighter in England. He took money from rich people and gave it to the poor villagers.

The most famous Robin Hood stories are in this book. They are about beautiful Lady Marian, the greedy Sheriff of Nottingham, good King Richard, and his bad brother, Prince John.

Many countries have stories about brave and clever adventurers. But is Robin Hood only a story? Perhaps Robin really did live, and perhaps not. There *was* a King Richard; he was king from 1189 to 1199. He left England and fought in Jerusalem. When he was away, Prince John was the most important man in England. Then, when Richard died, John was the next king.

The stories say that Robin Hood lived with his men in Sherwood Forest, near the town of Nottingham. Sherwood Forest and Nottingham are about two hundred kilometres north of London. Many people there say that Robin Hood really lived in the forest.

Chapter 1
Robin Fitzooth is Born in Sherwood Forest

The Robin Hood stories are very famous. Most people know that Robin lived in Saxon and Norman times. He robbed rich people and gave the money to poor people. But not everybody knows that he came from a rich family. And not many people know that Robin Hood was half-Saxon and half-Norman.

◆

The story begins with Robin Hood's Saxon grandfather, Sir★ George Gamwell. Gamwell lived near a Norman lord★. This lord wanted to take Gamwell's house and his lands. The two men fought, and the Norman lord killed Gamwell's two sons. Gamwell's wife also died.

But Sir George also had a young daughter, Joanna.

'I have no sons,' Gamwell said to Joanna. 'So I will teach you to fight with a sword, and with a bow and arrow.'

Five years later, Joanna was nineteen years old and very beautiful. One day, a young man visited Sir George. His name was William Fitzooth, and he was a Norman.

'Sir George,' he began, 'I love your daughter. I hope that she loves me. I would like to marry her. I have money and land . . .'

But Sir George was very angry.

'Never!' he answered. 'My daughter will never marry you. Get off my land. Do not come here again or I will kill you!'

Joanna loved this young man. So she tried to talk to her father, but he didn't want to listen.

★ Sir, Lord, Lady: Important men had the words *Sir* or *Lord* before their names; important women had the word *Lady*.

'Go to your room!' he shouted. 'I do not want to hear that man's name again.'

That night, William came back to Sir George's home. He stood under Joanna's window and called to her. Joanna took some clothes and came quietly out of the house.

William took her hand. 'Will you come with me and marry me?' he asked. 'We cannot live in my home because your father's men will look for you there. So we will live in the green forest.'

'I am sorry for my father,' Joanna said sadly, 'but I love you. I know you are a good man. I will marry you.'

In the morning, Sir George woke late. He called to his men, 'Where is my daughter? I want to speak to her.'

But Joanna was nowhere in the house.

Sir George was very angry, then very sad.

'I have no family now,' he thought.

◆

One fine day in April, a year later, a man came to the house.

'Your daughter sent me here,' he said. 'She wants you to come and see her.'

Sir George followed the man to the middle of Sherwood Forest. There, in the spring sunshine, he saw his daughter. He also saw a baby boy in her arms. Joanna looked up at her father and smiled.

'This is Robin, your grandson,' she said.

She gave the baby to her father. Sir George wanted to be angry, but he was very happy with his grandson in his arms.

'Robin? Is that your name?' he said. 'Well, little Robin, I wanted to kill your father but that is not possible now. Please, daughter, come with your husband and live near me. Let's forget the past.'

'We will come and live near you, father,' said Joanna. 'But I will often bring my son to the forest. I will teach him to find his way in the forest in the day and at night. He will learn to make arrows for his bow, and to catch forest animals. He will make a fire and cook the meat. The forest will always be his second home.'

Chapter 2
The Sheriff of Nottingham Finds Robin Hood

Robin's grandfather died, then his mother and father. After twenty-five years, Robin was lord of Gamwell and Locksley, and lived in his father's home, Locksley House.

The village people liked Robin Fitzooth.

'He is a good man,' they said. 'No man, woman or child is hungry on Robin of Locksley's lands.'

Not all lords were so kind. The worst person was the greedy Sheriff of Nottingham. The sheriff took everything from the villagers, and often these poor people were very hungry. Robin listened carefully to the stories about the sheriff. He sent food and clothes to the poorest families.

◆

At about this time, people began to tell stories about a robber. They called him Robin Hood.

'The sheriff is a hard man,' they said. 'He and his rich friends take everything from us. But now brave Robin Hood and his men rob rich people and give their money to poor villagers!'

In those days, the Great North Road went through Sherwood Forest. Robin Hood's men often stopped rich men in the forest, and took their money. Sometimes Prince John's men also used the road. So Robin Hood robbed him too.

'The forest is on your land,' said Prince John to the sheriff. 'Why don't you catch and kill this robber?'

'It is not so easy,' answered the sheriff. 'The village people don't want to tell me much. They say only that the robbers live in or near Sherwood Forest. But they know more than they say. I have a plan to learn more about this man Robin Hood.'

'What is your plan?' asked the prince.

'It is this,' answered the sheriff. 'Robin of Locksley lives near Sherwood Forest. Tonight there is going to be a great party at Locksley House. I know that Fitzooth will invite the village people on his land. So I will send one of my men. He can wear village clothes and ask questions about "good" Robin Hood, "the people's friend". When I know more about this Robin, I can catch him.'

That evening, there were a lot of people at Locksley House. There was food and drink for the villagers, and there was dancing and singing. Everybody was very happy. And Robin was the happiest person there, because he and the lovely Lady Marian Fitzwalter planned to marry the next day.

The sheriff's man turned to a villager next to him.

'I often hear the name Robin Hood,' he said. 'Who is he? Does he live near here?'

The man laughed. 'Don't you know, friend? Robin Fitzooth is Robin Hood!'

The sheriff's man quickly left Locksley House and went to his lord.

'This is better than I hoped,' said the sheriff. 'Tomorrow, Robin Fitzooth will marry Lady Marian at St Mary's Abbey. But my men will stop him and bring him to me. Prince John will kill him and give me Fitzooth's money and lands. Lady Marian's family is also rich. She will not marry Robin, so perhaps I will marry her. Yes, tomorrow will be a great day for me!'

Chapter 3   At St Mary's Abbey

At 10 o'clock the next morning, Robin Fitzooth and Lady Marian stood in front of the abbot in St Mary's Abbey. Lady Marian was some years younger than Robin, and very lovely. She wore a white dress, and her long hair was the colour of the forest trees in autumn.

The abbot began to speak.

'Robin of Locksley,' he began 'do you . . .'

'Stop!' somebody called from the back of the church. Robin turned. It was the Sheriff of Nottingham. Behind the sheriff were twenty men with bows and arrows.

'My Lord Abbot,' called the sheriff loudly. 'This man has to come with me. He is the robber, Robin Hood!' Then he turned to his men. 'Why are you waiting?' he asked. 'Take him!'

'Yes, I am Robin Hood,' answered Robin, 'but you will not take me. Look carefully round the church, Sheriff. Do you not see my men?'

The sheriff looked and saw thirty or more tall, strong men.

The abbot was angry and afraid. 'What are you doing?' he shouted. 'Will you fight in a church?'

'This man has to come with me,' said the sheriff again. 'Give me your sword, Robin Hood, and come quietly. The good abbot does not want you to fight!'

Robin walked slowly to the sheriff.

'Here you are, my Lord,' he said – and hit the sheriff hard on the head with the top of his sword. The sheriff fell back.

'Outside! Everybody outside!' shouted Robin.

His men pushed the sheriff's men back through the church door. A great fight began outside the abbey.

Robin spoke quickly to Marian.

'We can fight and win today,' he said. 'But now the sheriff knows my name, and I cannot go back to Locksley House. Wait for me, my love. King Richard will come back to England – he will hear about the greedy sheriff and his friends. But now I will be Robin Hood of Sherwood Forest and not Robin of Locksley. I will never hurt a woman, a child or a poor man. But rich and greedy men will be afraid to walk near my forest home!'

Chapter 4   The King's Deer

After the fight in the abbey, the Sheriff of Nottingham asked Prince John for Robin Fitzooth's lands. The prince sold them to him for a lot of money in gold. The greedy sheriff, of course, wanted to get the money back again as fast as possible. So his poor villagers had to pay the sheriff more money than before. The villagers on Robin's land also had to pay. Their new lord, the sheriff, was a very hard man.

One of these villages was Farnsfield. It was very close to Sherwood, and the villagers often went into the forest. There they caught small animals and birds for their dinner. On their first visit to Farnsfield, the sheriff and his men took money and food. They also found an old man in the forest, with a dead deer on his back.

That evening, the sheriff called all the villagers. Then his men brought out the old man and the dead deer.

'Listen well!' said the sheriff loudly. 'You know that the deer in the forest are the king's deer. The king and his lords can catch and kill them – you cannot. This evening, I will help you to remember that!'

The sheriff looked at the villagers and smiled. Nobody spoke. Then he turned to the old man.

'What is your name, old man?' asked the sheriff, coldly.

'I ... I ... I am Much the forester, My Lord,' answered the man, very afraid.

'Well, Much the forester,' said the sheriff. 'You killed a king's deer. How much are you going to pay me for it?'

'My Lord, you know that I cannot give you anything!' said poor Much. 'You ... you took our money ... and our food. I found the deer, but it was dead. I didn't kill it!'

'I am not interested in your stories, old man,' said the sheriff. 'You cannot pay me any money? Very well, then you will have to pay with your life!'

He turned to one of his men. 'Kill this robber,' he said, 'and pull down his home! This will be a lesson for the villagers of Farnsfield!'

The sheriff's man took out his sword, and pulled back Much's head. The villagers could not help the old forester because they were afraid. But Much called out, 'No! Kill me, but please do not pull down my house! It is my son's home, too, and he did not hurt you. *He* did not take the deer. Wait, please ...!' Much turned his eyes to the forest. 'Oh, Robin Hood,' he thought, 'where are you now? Only you can help me.'

'So you have a son?' said the sheriff's man. 'Well, he can stay in your house when we pull it down!'

He laughed loudly, but the sheriff looked more carefully at the forester.

'Wait!' he called. 'I think this man knows something! Old man, why are you looking into the forest? Do you think that Robin Hood will help you? Do you know something about him? Tell me, and perhaps I will not kill you!'

'I can take you to Robin Hood!' said Much quickly. 'I can take you to his home in the forest. It is this way! Follow me!'

The sheriff's man took his hands away, and Much began to move slowly to the forest. Then he suddenly ran as fast as he could.

'Catch him!' shouted the sheriff.

Much was nearly inside the forest now, but the sheriff's fighters quickly took out their bows. Three arrows hit him, and Much fell to the ground. His open eyes looked up at the sky.

'I said "catch him", not "kill him",' said the sheriff angrily. 'Now the man is dead, he cannot tell us anything.' He looked at the villagers again. 'Perhaps one of you can tell me the way through the forest to the robber's home? I will pay you well!'

But nobody told the sheriff about Robin Hood.

The sheriff was now very angry.

'There is nothing more for us here,' he said to his men. 'Pull down the forester's house, and we will go.'

He turned one last time to the villagers. 'The next man with a deer will die too – but not as quickly. Remember that!'

Later in the evening, the villagers carried Much into the centre of the village. The forester's young son stood outside his father's house. There was nothing there now.

'We are very sorry,' the villagers said to the boy. 'We could not do anything. Do not be too sad – your father died bravely!'

Then a small man with a bow and arrows on his back walked quietly into the village.

'It is Will Scarlet, Robin Hood's man!' said the villagers.

Will Scarlet put down his bow, and put his hand on the boy's head.

'Robin knows that the sheriff was here,' he said. 'He sent me to help, but I am too late! Who was this man? Was he your father?'

'Yes, he was my father,' answered the young boy sadly. 'Now I have no family – and no home!' He turned to Will Scarlet. 'Oh, please,' he cried, 'take me with you! My father taught me a lot about the forest. You can teach me to be a fighter too! I want to be Robin Hood's man. I want to fight the sheriff – and Prince John too.'

'You are very young,' said Will. 'When you are older, perhaps . . .'

'I am not young, I am fourteen,' said the boy. 'I am small, but I am strong. I learn quickly. I have nothing here. Please take me with you.'

And so Will Scarlet took young Much to Robin Hood.

That year, many young men came to the forest. They all had stories about the sheriff and his men. Robin and Will Scarlet taught them to use a sword and a bow and arrow. But Much, the forester's son, was always one of the best and bravest of Robin's men.

Chapter 5   Robin Hood Meets Little John

Our drink is strong, our food is good
Come in and drink with Robin Hood.
When Robin Hood is not at home
Come in and drink with Little John.
        (An old drinking song)

In the first weeks and months after the fight in the abbey, Robin and his men worked very hard. They cut down young trees and built homes in the centre of the forest. They made arrows from wood and caught forest deer for their food. They bought bread and milk from the villagers.

Sometimes Robin liked to leave his men, and look for adventure. One fine autumn morning, he and his friend Will Scarlet woke early.

'It is a beautiful day,' said Robin. 'I think I will go for a walk to the river. Will you come with me?'

'I want to make some new arrows for my bow,' answered Will. 'But I will meet you at lunch time near the bridge.'

So Robin left Will and walked quickly through the forest to the river and the little bridge. Robin stood in the middle of the bridge, and looked up at the trees.

'The autumn colours are beautiful,' he thought. Then he looked down at the water. 'I will catch a fish for our lunch,' he thought. 'Will and I can make a fire. I have some bread, and there is fruit on the trees. We will eat very well. Ah, this is a wonderful life!'

Suddenly somebody behind him said, 'Well, little man! Are you going to stand there all day? Get out of my way!'

Robin turned. The speaker was a big man, nearly two metres tall. 'Now this will be an interesting adventure,' he thought. 'That man is very strong. Can I fight him – and win?' He did not move from the bridge.

'I arrived here first,' he called to the big man, 'so you will have to wait. I think I am going to do some fishing. Then, perhaps, I will get out of your way.'

The big man moved onto the bridge.

'I will not wait!' he said. 'And you are not going to fish, you are going to fight!'

They fought there, in the middle of the bridge. Robin couldn't win. He knew that after a minute or two. The man wasn't very fast but he was *very* strong. So Robin quickly thought of a plan.

He looked over the top of the big man's head, and shouted, 'Look, the sheriff's men!'

The big man turned and looked. Robin quickly kicked the man's legs as hard as he could. The big man was very angry – but he didn't fall. He kicked Robin, and Robin fell off the bridge into the water.

The big man laughed.

'I won the fight,' he said. 'Come, I will help you.'

He looked over the bridge into the water. But Robin was not there.

'Where are you?' called the man. 'Are you all right?'

Robin suddenly came up from the water. He was a long way from the bridge.

'Perhaps you won the fight,' laughed Robin, 'but you did not catch me!'

He began to climb onto dry ground. Then Will Scarlet arrived.

They fought there, in the middle of the bridge.

'What happened, Robin?' he called. 'Did this man throw you in the water? He will have to fight me now!'

'No! No!' laughed Robin. 'Let's be friends. So what is your name, friend? And what are you doing in my forest?'

'*Your* forest?' answered the big man. 'It is not your forest! I came here to find brave Robin Hood. But first, I think, I will throw you in the river again!'

'Friend,' said Robin, 'you found Robin Hood, *and* threw him in the water. Please, don't do it again!'

'What! Are you really Robin Hood?' asked the man. 'I am very happy about that. My name is John Little and I want to be one of your men.'

Robin laughed. '"Little" is a good name for you, because you are very small – only the size of a small tree! We will always call you our "little" John. Come to our forest home, Little John!'

Chapter 6   Robin Hood Helps Sir Richard of Lee

Autumn went and winter came. One cold but sunny day in January, a man came slowly over the Great North Road on an old horse. The snow on the forest trees shone in the winter sunshine. But the man did not look at the forest. He looked only at the road in front of him.

'It is a beautiful morning,' he heard suddenly. 'Why are you so sad?'

Will Scarlet came out of the forest and stood in the middle of the road. The man looked up.

'Who are you?' he asked.

'My name is Will Scarlet,' said Will, 'and I am Robin Hood's man. Are you afraid?'

'No, I am not afraid,' said the man. 'I know that Robin Hood helps poor people. But he cannot help me.'

Will Scarlet laughed.

'Perhaps we can help you, and perhaps we can't. Robin Hood and his men love dangerous adventures. Come and eat with us! Tell us your problems!'

So Will Scarlet took the man to Robin Hood. First, they gave him food and drink. He was very hungry.

'You eat well in your forest home,' said the man. 'You eat as well as the King – perhaps better! Thank you for this good food.'

Then he stood up.

'Wait,' said Robin. 'Can't you pay us something for your dinner? With a little gold I can help many poor families.'

The man did not answer for some time.

Then he said, 'I have gold in my bags – six hundred pounds! But I cannot give it to you. I am going to St Mary's Abbey. This money is for the abbot.'

'That is a lot of money,' said Will, 'and the church has too much gold.'

'That is my problem,' said the man. 'The abbot wants more – five hundred pounds more – and I cannot pay him this year. Perhaps he will wait another year, but I think not. I think that he will ask for my lands – and my home too.'

'Yes,' said Robin, 'the abbot is a greedy man. Tell us your name, friend, and tell us your story too. Perhaps we can help.'

So the man told his story. His name was Richard of Lee, and his son killed a man in a fight. The man died, and the Sheriff of Nottingham's men took the boy away.

'Ah, the sheriff,' said Robin. 'Another greedy man! Did he ask for money?'

'You know him well,' answered Richard of Lee. 'He said, "Pay me one thousand pounds or your son will die!" I am not a rich man, but the Abbot of St Mary's paid the money for me. This happened last year. Now I have to pay the abbot. He wants one thousand, one hundred pounds – and I can only give him six hundred.'

Robin laughed. 'I can give you the money. But first, let's try something ... perhaps the good abbot is not a bad man. Tell him that you do not have the money. Ask him to help you. Ask him to wait another year!'

Then Robin turned to his men.

'Who will go with this man and listen to the abbot's answer?'

'I will go with him,' said Little John. 'I am ready for an adventure!'

Chapter 7   Sir Richard Pays the Abbot

At twelve o'clock the next day, the Abbot of St Mary's was in his great dining room. On the table there were bags of gold. He went to the window and looked out.

'Sir Richard of Lee is here at the right time, I see,' he thought. 'But his clothes are poor, and his horse is old. Good! I think my friend, the sheriff, is right. Sir Richard cannot pay my one thousand, one hundred pounds. So this evening, I will be Lord of his house and his lands!'

A few minutes later, Sir Richard and Little John came into the room.

'Well,' said the abbot, 'you are here at the right time. Do you have my money?'

'My Lord Abbot,' Sir Richard began, 'you are a church man. I hope you will be kind. Next year . . .'

'Stop!' shouted the abbot. 'Do not ask for more time! I want my money now. Pay me the one thousand, one hundred pounds, or your house and lands will be mine this evening!'

Sir Richard then put six bags of gold on the abbot's table. 'Here are six hundred pounds, My Lord,' he said quietly. 'There is one hundred in each bag. It is a lot of money for me. Next year I hope ...'

'Not next year, or next month, or next week!' shouted the abbot again. 'I want all my money today! Do you have my gold – yes or no?'

Then Little John put five more bags on the table.

'Here you are, My Lord,' he said. 'Five hundred more pounds. This good man and his family will sleep in their home tonight.'

The abbot looked at the money, then he looked at Little John. The abbot's face was very red. He opened his mouth and then closed it again. What could he say?

Later, in the forest, Little John told the story to Robin Hood and the other men.

'The abbot's face was wonderful,' said Little John. 'He was angry, but he had to take the money.'

They laughed for a long time, but then Robin said,

'This was a fine adventure. But the abbot will tell the sheriff, and the sheriff will also be angry. They are dangerous men. Sir Richard has to be careful.'

Chapter 8
Lady Marian and the Sheriff of Nottingham

Every year in summer, Marian's father had a great party. Lords and ladies and the people from the villages came. They ate and drank. This year, the Sheriff of Nottingham came too, with fifty of his men. He watched Marian carefully.

'She is very beautiful,' he thought, 'and Robin Hood loves her. I know he will come today. Then my men can catch him.'

The music started and people began to dance. A man went to Marian and spoke to her. She smiled and gave him her hand.

The sheriff stood up and called loudly to his men, 'That's him! That's Robin Hood! Take him!'

15

Then Little John put five more bags on the table.

The sheriff's men took out their swords and moved through the dancers. Suddenly ten of the dancers ran for their swords too. They were, of course, Robin's men, and a great fight began. Robin's men were better fighters than the sheriff's. Marian wanted to fight too, but her father stopped her.

'Marian, what are you doing? Put down that sword! I am sorry about Robin – no other man will marry you. You are only interested in fighting!'

The sheriff heard Marian's father and smiled.

'Lady Marian is really very lovely,' he thought. 'Her father wants to find another husband for her? Good. I will marry her, then she will help me find Robin Hood.'

Chapter 9   The Sheriff's Visit

The next day, the sheriff arrived at Lord Fitzwalter's house with twenty horsemen. Lord Fitzwalter watched them through a window. He was not happy.

'He wants to talk about yesterday's fight,' he said to his daughter, 'and you nearly fought too! Please go to your room. I will speak to him.'

'I do not want to speak to the sheriff, father,' said Marian, 'but I will listen behind the door!'

Marian left the room, and a minute later, the sheriff walked in.

'My Lord Sheriff,' began Lord Fitzwalter, 'I am sorry about the fight yesterday, but your men . . .'

'No, no, I do not want to talk about that,' said the sheriff. He put his hand on Lord Fitzwalter's arm and smiled. 'I want to speak to you about your daughter, the Lady Marian.'

'Ah, Marian,' said Lord Fitzwalter unhappily. 'Marian is a good girl but she does not always listen to me. Perhaps one day a husband will . . .'

'Ah yes!' said the sheriff and smiled. 'Well, I am looking for a wife, and I would like to marry your daughter. I like a strong woman – and Marian is also very beautiful. I will be a good husband. I have lands, money – and important friends.'

'My Lord, what can I say?' said Marian's father. He was now very unhappy. Marian wanted to marry Robin and no other man – he knew that. 'You are very kind. I will talk to Marian but ...'

'I will come back tomorrow,' said the sheriff. 'Remember – Prince John is my very good friend. He can be your friend too. Think carefully!'

◆

That evening, Marian and her father talked for a long time about Robin, the sheriff and Prince John.

'Marian, why don't you marry the sheriff?' said her father. 'He is rich and important, and he is a friend of Prince John. I am afraid of the prince. Please marry the sheriff, and forget Robin Fitzooth.'

Marian took her father's hand. 'Father, I am sorry to bring you so many problems. I will not marry the sheriff, but he will be angry with me, not you. Listen. Tomorrow I will leave the house very early and stay with my uncle. The sheriff will come late in the morning. Tell your men to look for me. Look in every room. Be very angry. Then the sheriff will think that you know nothing!'

'You are right, Marian,' said her father. 'You will have to marry the sheriff or leave here. Go then to my brother's house. But who will go with you?'

'Good Friar Tuck is staying here tonight,' answered Marian. 'He will help me.'

'That fat churchman?' said her father. 'He is a strange friar. He fights too well for a churchman. People say that the Abbot of St Mary's hates him. The friar had to leave the abbey.'

'Friar Tuck does not like the abbot because the abbot takes a lot of money from the villagers,' answered Marian. 'Friar Tuck says that the church has to help poor people.'

'Mm,' said her father. 'The abbot does live very well. He is a greedy man. Friar Tuck is greedy too – he eats more than ten men! But he is a brave man and very strong. Yes, take Friar Tuck with you.'

Chapter 10   Marian Goes to Sherwood Forest

Very early next morning, Marian put on boy's clothes and a boy's hat and woke up Friar Tuck. The friar took his staff and Marian took her bow and arrows. Then they left the house and walked on the Great North Road through the forest.

After some hours, the friar suddenly left the road and sat down under a tree.

'Please let's stop, My Lady,' he said. 'We had no breakfast and I am very hungry!'

Marian laughed.

'I am sorry, Friar Tuck,' she said. 'You are right, we will eat now. Stay here. I will take your staff and my bow and arrow, and catch some animals. We can cook them here in the forest.'

Marian left the friar and moved quietly between the forest trees. She saw a deer. Very quietly, she took out an arrow and put it to her bow.

'Stop there, boy!' said a man behind her. The man spoke very loudly. The deer jumped at the noise and ran away into the trees. Marian was very angry. She turned to the speaker but he wore a big hood. She couldn't see his face.

'Well, boy,' said the man. 'Don't you know that you cannot eat the king's deer? The Sheriff of Nottingham killed two men last week because they caught a deer.'

'I am not afraid of the sheriff,' said Marian, 'or of you. Leave now – or fight!'

'Fight with you?' the man laughed. 'But you are only a boy! Well, you have a staff and I have one too. I will fight with you – with one hand!'

Marian fought well. She was strong and quick. With only one hand, the man could not win. She hit him again and again on his head and across his back.

'Stop, stop!' he laughed. 'You are young, but you are a good fighter.' He threw back his hood. 'I am Robin Hood. Will you come with me, and be one of my men?'

'Robin!' said Marian, and threw back her hood too. Her lovely red hair fell down her back.

'Marian!' answered Robin. 'What are you doing here, in the forest? Is nobody with you?'

'I am with a friend, Friar Tuck,' said Marian, 'and he is very hungry! The deer was for him. But I think that he will be happy to eat at Robin Hood's table.'

She and Robin went back to the road and looked for Friar Tuck. They called his name but there was no answer.

'Poor man!' said Marian. 'Perhaps he is looking for me. Perhaps he thinks that the sheriff's men caught me!'

Then she told Robin about her father and the sheriff.

'I cannot go home now, Robin,' she said. 'I want to be with you here, in Sherwood Forest. Friar Tuck will marry us. Let's find him. Perhaps he will want to live with us.'

Chapter 11   Robin Hood and Friar Tuck

They did not find Friar Tuck that day, so Marian stayed with her uncle. She came each day to the forest.

'Another friar lives at my uncle's home,' she told Robin, 'but he is a weak man. He doesn't want to marry us because he is

'Robin!' said Marian, and threw back her hood.

afraid. And the sheriff will find me at my uncle's house. Oh, where is Friar Tuck? Only he can help us.'

◆

Then one day, about a month after the fight between Marian and Robin, Will Scarlet told them an interesting story.

'People in the village of River Dale are talking about a fat friar,' he said. 'They say he came to the village last month. Now he lives near the river. For one penny, he will take people across the river in his boat. When poor people cannot pay, he carries them across on his back! People say he loves good food and a good fight. He is a very strange friar, I think.'

'And I think that man is Friar Tuck,' laughed Marian. 'Robin, please go to River Dale and bring him back with you.'

Robin and Will Scarlet walked with Marian to her uncle's house and then went back through the forest to the village of River Dale.

'Wait here, Will,' said Robin. 'Marian says the friar is a strong man and very brave. I'd like to try him!'

Robin then walked to the river and looked across it. He saw the friar's little house, and his boat.

'Good friar,' he called, 'where are you? Will you take me in your boat? I have some money and I can pay you well.'

Friar Tuck came out of the house and got into the boat. He came quickly across the river.

'Show me your money first,' said the friar. 'Then you can get in.'

He jumped from the boat to dry ground and held out his hand. Robin gave him a penny and walked to the boat. But he didn't get in. He pushed the boat and it moved slowly away, down the river.

'You stupid man! What are you doing?' shouted Friar Tuck.

Robin took out his sword.

'Now we have no boat, friar,' he said. 'Carry me across the river on your back and perhaps I will not kill you!'

The friar said nothing. He looked at Robin's sword and then walked into the water. Robin climbed onto his back and they went slowly to the middle of the river. Then the friar suddenly stopped, stood up, and threw Robin into the water.

Friar Tuck could swim more quickly than Robin. He got out of the river and called,

'Come here, friend, and fight with me. I do not have a sword because I am a churchman. And I can kill a man with my two hands!'

Then Will Scarlet came out of the forest with ten of Robin's men.

'Robin, are you hurt?' he called. Robin climbed out of the river.

'What are you going to do now, friar?' said Robin. 'Will you fight us?'

Friar Tuck did not answer him. He called loudly, 'Hunter! Biter! Here, my boys!'

Two great dogs came out of the forest.

'My two dogs and I are ready to fight you!' said Friar Tuck. 'But tell me first, are you Robin Hood?'

'I am,' said Robin. 'Lady Marian sent me. She is right – you are a good fighter! Will you come and live in the forest? Will you be our friar?'

The next day, Friar Tuck married Robin and Marian in the little church of River Dale. Then he left his house by the river. Now he was one of Robin's men.

The friar looked at Robin's sword and then walked into the water.

Chapter 12
The Two Churchmen and the Bags of Gold

Another winter came and went. There was not much snow on the ground and people could again use the Great North Road.

'One day, Sir Richard of Lee will pay us the abbot's money,' said Robin to Little John and Will Scarlet. 'But perhaps we can get the money back from the church first.'

'A good plan, Robin,' answered Little John. 'I will find a rich churchman and invite him to a forest dinner. Then he can pay us five hundred pounds. That is not too expensive for our best forest deer, our whitest bread and our finest wine!'

◆

The next evening, Little John went to the road and waited at the robbers' usual place behind a tree. He didn't have to wait long. Two churchmen on beautiful white horses were on the road. The two men wore expensive clothes. They were afraid, and they often looked into the forest.

Little John came out of the forest and moved to the middle of the road.

'Good evening, brothers,' he called. 'Are you going to St Mary's Abbey?'

They stopped their horses and the younger churchman answered, 'Yes, we are going to visit the abbot. Are we near the abbey? We don't want to be on this road at night. People say robbers live in the forests near here!'

'I am the abbot's man,' said Little John. 'I can show you a quick way to the abbey. Follow me!'

So the two men followed Little John into the forest. After a few minutes they saw smoke and then a fire. Robin's men were there.

'Where are we?' cried the churchmen. 'Who are these men? This is not the abbey!'

'Good evening, brothers!' said Robin. 'Don't be afraid, we will not hurt you. We hope you will stay for dinner!'

The two churchmen were very unhappy but they could not leave. So they got down from their horses and sat at Robin's table. Robin's men brought them meat, wine and bread. The food was very good, but the churchmen couldn't eat. They were too afraid.

'Not hungry?' asked Robin. 'Please eat more because we will ask you to pay something for your dinner. With a little church gold, we can help the abbot's villagers. On the abbot's land there are many poor families.'

The men's faces were very white. 'We are only poor churchmen,' they answered, 'and we have no money. Please don't kill us!'

Little John went to the churchmen's horses and looked in their bags. Then he called to Robin Hood.

'They are right, Robin. There is no money in their bags.'

'We told you that,' said one of the men. 'Please – it is very late and we want to get to the abbey. My Lord Abbot is waiting for us.'

'Wait!' answered Robin. 'You are wearing some fine clothes. You can pay for your dinner with those. Take them off!'

'What? Here, in the forest?' asked the men. 'The night is very cold!'

'Take them off,' Robin repeated, 'or do you want me to help you?' He took out his sword. The two men slowly took off all their clothes.

The robbers looked at the churchmen and began to laugh ... Under their clothes, each man had five large money bags.

'Look at that,' said Little John. 'What do we have here? Aha! There is gold in these bags! One hundred pounds in each bag.'

'We will take this gold,' said Robin Hood. 'It is not yours because you didn't have any money. Perhaps somebody put the gold there! Go now and tell the good abbot. Robin Hood found one thousand pounds!'

The two men began to put on their clothes again.

'No, no,' said Robin. 'You can give us your clothes too – and your horses. You can wear our old clothes, and walk to the abbey.'

The two men ran away and Robin Hood's men laughed for a long time.

'I would like to see the abbot's face tomorrow!' said Little John. 'This is more money than we gave him. He will not be a happy man.'

Chapter 13
Sir Richard of Lee Comes Back to the Forest

The next day, Sir Richard arrived.

'Robin, my good friend,' he said, 'I have your money, and I am also bringing one hundred arrows for you and your men. My wife and her friends made them.'

'You are a good man,' Robin answered. 'We are very happy about the arrows, but I will not take your gold. The abbot took that money last year – and yesterday the church gave it back to me!'

He told Sir Richard about the two churchmen and the bags of gold under their clothes.

'Now,' said Robin, 'I would like to give you and your lady something. I would like to give your wife this beautiful white horse. And for you, I have some fine clothes!'

The two churchmen arrived at the abbey later the next day and also told their story. The abbot was very angry.

'Robin Hood is laughing now,' he said, 'but one day, the sheriff or I will kill him for this.'

Chapter 14 Robin Hood and the Gold Arrow

Every day, the sheriff's men brought new stories about Robin Hood. Prince John heard the stories too.

'This man Robin Hood only has fifty men,' he said to the sheriff. 'You have five hundred men but you cannot catch him. People are laughing at you! What are you going to do?'

'I have another plan, My Lord,' said the sheriff. 'I will have a contest with bows and arrows. The winner will get a gold arrow. I know that Robin Hood will come. Everybody says that he is the best bowman in England. He will win the contest and take the gold arrow. Then I will take him.'

◆

Robin and his men heard about the contest. The sheriff was right – they wanted to go.

'You will have to stay at home, Robin,' laughed Little John. 'We want to win, and we are better than the sheriff's men. But you are a better bowman than all of us!'

'Be careful, Robin,' said Marian. 'The sheriff is a dangerous man. He knows that you will go. He only wants to find you and kill you!'

'I know that,' said Robin. 'This is a fine adventure. I will win the contest, but the sheriff won't catch me . . .'

'Then I will come too,' said Marian. 'I will wear boy's clothes again, and my boy's hat. The sheriff will not know me, and I will play in the contest. Perhaps I will win the gold arrow, not you!'

◆

On the day of the contest, many people came. Some people played and other people watched. One hundred of the sheriff's men were there too.

'The winner of this contest will be Robin Hood,' the sheriff told his men. 'He will come to take the gold arrow from me –

then you can take him. But do not kill him. Prince John wants to meet him first!'

The contest began. One man was the best.

'That man is Robin Hood,' thought the Sheriff. 'People say he is clever. But we will catch him easily. That big man with him is Little John and the fat man is Friar Tuck. We will take them too. But who is the boy? He is very good with a bow and arrow too.'

The contest finished and Robin Hood was the winner. He went to the sheriff and smiled.

'The arrow is mine, I think,' he said. The sheriff smiled coldly and gave him the gold arrow. Then Robin turned away.

'Take him now!' shouted the sheriff to his men.

But twenty of Robin's men took off their hoods and moved behind Robin. A great swordfight began. Robin's men and the sheriff's fought for a long time. Marian fought too this time, and she fought well. Many of the sheriff's men died that day. The sheriff was very angry.

'Where are Prince John's men?' he shouted. 'They are late, and Robin Hood is winning!'

Then Prince John arrived with fifty men on horses.

'They are too many,' called Robin to his men, 'and they are on horses. Get back to the forest! Marian, come!'

Then Will Scarlet called out, 'Robin, Marian! They hurt Little John!'

'Don't wait for me,' said Little John. 'It is my leg. I cannot walk. Go! Go!'

'Never!' said Robin.

With Will and Marian's help, he put Little John on his back and ran to the forest road. Suddenly a man arrived on a white horse. It was Richard of Lee.

'Quick, Robin, put Little John on the horse and follow me. The sheriff and his men will not look for you in my home!' So

'That man is Robin Hood,' thought the Sheriff.

Sir Richard helped his friends Robin, Marian, Little John and Will Scarlet. They stayed at Sir Richard's house that night. Robin told Sir Richard and his wife about the contest and about other adventures in the forest.

'You have many adventures, My Lady,' said Sir Richard's wife to Marian, 'but you live dangerously. You cannot go home or visit your father. How will these adventures end? When will you leave the forest?'

'One day, King Richard will come home,' answered Marian. 'Then life will be better for poor people and Robin and I will go home.'

Chapter 15   The Tall Friar

People loved King Richard because he was a brave man and a good king. But his brother, Prince John, only wanted to be king and to be rich. People hated him.

When King Richard was in England, the prince and other important Norman lords had to listen to their king. They could not take land and money from weaker men. But Richard fought in Jerusalem for many years. When the king was away, Prince John and his friends were greedy and unkind.

Then, one day, the prince got a letter from the Sheriff of Nottingham.

'My Lord Prince,' wrote the sheriff, 'the people are saying that your brother Richard is here in the North. They say he is going from town to town and asking questions about me – and about you. We will have to be very careful . . .'

'So,' thought the prince, 'Richard is in England again. Why isn't he dead? And why didn't he come here to London? What stories about me is he listening to? I think I too will go to Nottingham and visit my friend the sheriff. Perhaps he can tell me more.'

So the prince took the Great North Road to the sheriff's house. A hundred strong men went with him. They took the road through Sherwood Forest, and there they met a churchman. The man was very tall and strong and he wore a great hood over his face.

'Well, friar,' said the prince, 'you are a brave man. Is nobody with you? Aren't you afraid? Don't you know that the robber, Robin Hood, lives in Sherwood Forest?'

'People say that Robin Hood does not hurt poor men,' said the friar.

'People say stupid things,' answered the prince angrily. 'They say that my brother Richard is in England. But I say that he is dead! I will be king then. Now move out of my way!'

The tall man moved out of the way of the horses. He looked back at Prince John and his men for some minutes. Then he left the road and walked quickly into the forest. The tall man walked for a long time. Evening came. Then he heard something up in the trees:

'Good evening, brother. Why are you walking in the forest? Is nobody with you? Are you not afraid?'

The tall man laughed.

'Another person asked me that question. I am not afraid. I am looking for Robin Hood.'

Will Scarlet jumped down lightly from the tree.

'Then I will take you to him,' he said.

When they arrived in the middle of the forest, Robin's men were there. There was good food on the tables again.

'Robin!' called Will. 'This good friar wants to meet you.'

'We want to meet him too,' said Robin. 'We will eat with rich men, but we ask them to pay for their dinner. Poor people pay us with their stories. What is your story, friend? Why do you want to meet me?'

'This is my story,' said the friar. 'I left England with King Richard. Now the king is in England again, and I came too.

'What is your story, friend? Why do you want to meet me?'

People everywhere tell me stories about Robin Hood, so I wanted to meet you.'

'Oh, Robin,' said Marian, 'this is wonderful. The king is here in England! Let's go and find him. We can tell him everything about the sheriff and Prince John . . .'

'I love no man in the world more than the king,' said Robin. 'But what will he think? His brother is a greedy man. I can tell him that. But Prince John will say I am a robber. I think, for now, that I will stay quiet.'

The tall churchman stood up.

'You are wrong, Robin,' he said. Then he called loudly, 'To me! To me!'

Suddenly fifty strong men came out of the dark night and stood behind him.

'What is this?' said Robin. 'Are you Prince John's man? Are the prince and his men here? Are they really so brave?'

'Perhaps my brother is not a brave man. But I am Richard, your king, and I wanted to meet the famous Robin Hood. I hear many good stories about you, Robin. And other people also tell me bad stories about my brother. I know that John gave your lands to the sheriff. But from today, you will be Robin of Locksley again, and the king's friend.'

Chapter 16   The Last Adventure

After his visit to Sherwood Forest, King Richard went back to London. Robin and his men left the forest. Will Scarlet went to London with the king, but Little John stayed with Robin and Marian at Locksley House.

◆

One day, two years later, Robin visited his old friend, Friar Tuck. They talked for a long time about their adventures.

'I eat too well now, Robin,' said the friar. 'I am too fat and I cannot fight. People say that King Richard is ill. I hope that he will live for a long time. I hope that John will never be king. I wouldn't like to sleep on a hard bed in the forest again!'

On the way home, Robin walked slowly and thought about Friar Tuck's words. Then he heard the noise of horses' feet on the road, and looked up. It was the sheriff and his men.

'Robin Fitzooth,' called the sheriff, 'I have here a letter from the king. It says that you will come with me!'

'From King Richard?' asked Robin. 'Why does the king send *you*? He knows that we are not friends!'

The sheriff came nearer, but not too near. He was very afraid of Robin.

'Not King Richard,' he answered. 'Richard is dead! I am talking about King John. Take him, men!'

Robin pulled out his sword and began to fight. At the same time he moved slowly away from the road to the forest. There were too many men – he couldn't win. He had cuts on his right arm, and the arm hurt very badly.

When he got to the forest, he ran. He could find his way through forest very well, and the sheriff's men lost him.

Robin went through the forest to St Mary's Abbey. In front of the abbey, he fell to the ground. There, the abbot's men found him.

'It is Robin Hood!' said the abbot. 'I would like to kill him, but this is a church. Take him to one of the bedrooms. You, man, go to the sheriff. Tell him that Robin Hood is at the abbey.'

◆

Robin woke up. There was nobody in the room. He was very weak and couldn't move from the bed. Then he heard a friend.

'I am coming, Robin!' called Little John. 'Where are you?'

'Here! I am here!' said Robin weakly.

Little John broke open the door.

Robin spoke very slowly.

'Little John, help me one last time. Carry me to the window. Good. Now give me your bow.'

Little John helped Robin to put an arrow in the bow. They pulled. The arrow flew a long way, into the forest.

'Take me to that place and put me in the ground there,' said Robin.

There is a place in the forest near the abbey. There you can find these words:

Under this stone is Robin Hood.
Remember Robin and his men –
No braver man will come again.

ACTIVITIES

Chapters 1–5

Before you read

1 Robin Hood took money from rich people and gave it to people without money. How did he do it? Why did he do it? What do you think?

2 Find these words in your dictionary. They are all in the story.

abbey   abbot   arrow   bow   deer   forest   king   land   prince sheriff   sword

   a Find words for
- people
- places
- an animal

   b What did people use when they fought?

3 Answer the questions. Find the words in *italics* in your dictionary.

   a Which would you like to be?

     brave   greedy   poor

   b When John *robs* David, who loses?

   c Why do people like *adventures*?

   d What can you do with *gold*?

After you read

4 Why is:

   a Lord Gamwell first angry and sad, and then happy?

   b Prince John angry?

   c the abbot angry and afraid?

   d young Much sad and angry?

5 In the fight between Robin and Little John, who is stronger? Who is cleverer?

6 How is the story of Robin's parents the same as Shakespeare's story of *Romeo and Juliet*? How is it different? Talk about it.

Chapters 6–10

Before you read

7 How many of Robin Hood's men do you know? What do you know about them?

8 What are a *hood* and a *staff* in your language? Which do you carry in your hand? Which do you put on your head?

After you read

9 Finish these sentences. Put in the right number of pounds.
One year, the Abbot of St Mary's gave Richard of Lee £..... . The next year, Sir Richard had to pay the abbot £..... . But he only had £....., so Robin Hood gave him £..... .

10 Talk about Marian and her father. Who is braver? Why?

11 What do you think about Friar Tuck? Is he a good churchman? Why (not)?

Chapters 11–16

Before you read

12 What do you remember about Richard of Lee's story? Why will he come back to Sherwood Forest?

13 Will Robin and Marian marry? Will they live happily in the forest? What possible problems are there for them? What do you think?

14 What happens in a *contest*? Look in your dictionary.

After you read

15 Answer these questions.
a Why does Friar Tuck throw Robin in the river?
b What three things does Robin take from the churchmen? Who does he give them to?
c Who is the tall friar? Why is he on the Great North Road?
d How does the sheriff catch Robin Hood?

16 At the end of the story, have you got any questions? What would you like to know?

Writing

17 Work with other students. Make pictures of the people in the Robin Hood adventures, and write about them. Put your work up on your classroom wall.

18 Choose one adventure in this book, and tell the story.

19 It is a year after the end of the story. What is Marian doing now? Write a letter from her to a friend.

20 Write about an adventurer from your country. When did they live? What did they do? Who were they with? Who tried to stop them?

Answers for the Activities in this book are published in our free resource packs for teachers, the Penguin Readers Factsheets, or available on a separate sheet. Please write to your local Pearson Education office or to: Marketing Department, Penguin Longman Publishing, 5 Bentinck Street, London W1M 5RN.